Takin' It to the Streets

2004-2005 NMI
MISSION EDUCATION RESOURCES

❖ ❖ ❖

READING BOOKS

A DANGEROUS DEVOTION
Ordinary People in Extraordinary Adventures
by Carol Anne Eby

AFRICAN MOONS
by Juanita Moon

BEHIND THE VEIL
Taking Christ to Pakistanis
by Dallas Mucci

THE ROOKIE
Reflections of a New Missionary
by Tim Crutcher

TAKIN' IT TO THE STREETS
by Joe Colaizzi

WORDS OF LIFE AND LOVE
World Mission Literature Ministries
by Keith Schwanz

❖ ❖ ❖

ADULT MISSION EDUCATION RESOURCE BOOK

THE MISSION CALL
Edited by Wes Eby

Takin' It to the Streets

to
the
Streets

Joe Colaizzi

NPH

Nazarene Publishing House
Kansas City, Missouri

ISBN 083-412-0836

Printed in the United States of America

Editor: Wes Eby
Cover Design: Mike Walsh

10 9 8 7 6 5 4 3 2 1

Contents

Acknowledgments

To the Lord Jesus Christ,
my wife, Marilyn,
our children, Joey and Janna,
and each person named within these pages,
without whom there would be no story.

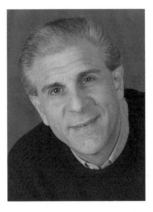

Joe Colaizzi, an ordained elder in the Church of the Nazarene, serves as director of the Kansas City Rescue Mission. Joe and his family reside in the Kansas City area.

Prologue

God calls each of us to a journey of faith.
He alone knows what will be required
to shape us for His appointed place of service.

The following is one man's story.

1
The Unpardonable Sin

The headline screamed: "Satan Is Alive and Well—Living Among Us!" Below the words, glaring hatefully through empty evil eyes, stood an artist's rendition of the devil—pitchfork in one hand, razor-sharp tail in the other.

The article described me well: "Self-centered and proud, angry and full of hate, cold-hearted, fearful, and rebellious."

How had this happened? How had I come to this? With each sentence, my greatest fear was further confirmed—I, Joe Colaizzi, was Satan!

■ ■ ■

It hadn't always been like this. An Italian Catholic heritage had led to 12 years of parochial schooling. The training had been top-notch, enviable to many. I'd even considered the priesthood. But a passion for independence and my attraction to the opposite sex was too compelling. Then there was Dolly, high school sweetheart.

Following high school, my search for purpose led to a junior college experiment with journalism

Joe's photo *(second from top on far right)*
appears on a Mister Rogers' Neighborhood Collage.

followed by a fine arts degree in radio and television from the University of Cincinnati. Shortly after graduation I secured a position with public television station WQED in my hometown of Pittsburgh. One of my first assignments was to assist with the production of the children's program *Mister Rogers' Neighborhood*.

After a semester of graduate school at Indiana University and a year as studio supervisor at WHAS-TV in Louisville, Kentucky, I returned to WQED and tied the knot with Dolly. Life was exciting.

Everything seemed great. I was on my way to a successful career. But something wasn't right. Somewhere, somehow, it all began to unravel.

Dolly had taken her vows seriously. I, on the other hand, found it easy to take her for granted and began to reach beyond the sacred boundaries of marriage into the forbidden area of promiscuity.

Peer pressure? Perhaps, but the choices were my own. Those "innocent" after-work visits to the bar, the drinks, the late nights, the first touch, the lies, and a hundred other foolish choices all had drawn me away from what I once knew to be right and now only pretended to believe.

After three years of marriage to this stranger who'd betrayed her, Dolly had had enough. I was devastated by the divorce! Wounded, I searched anxiously for answers. Rock music, maidens, and marijuana promised escape but led deceptively to a self-righteous pride, convincing me I had done no wrong and triggering within me a false sense of security that insisted life would work out to my advantage no matter what I did.

I quit my job at the TV station. Surely fate would see me through. But my funds quickly disappeared along with my self-confidence.

I panicked. It wasn't supposed to be this way. Nervously I sought employment, anywhere, everywhere. The hardware store lasted only days; I was too confused and unsure. The tree surgery job ended after six weeks. Fear and insecurity began to choke me.

■ ■ ■ ■ ■ ■

My sights were brazen:
to snatch the title "God."

■ ■ ■ ■ ■ ■

I stumbled into an entry-level position with a local film company where I stayed until I learned of a newly created position, director of instructional television, at Carnegie Mellon University. With borrowed courage and counterfeit confidence, I applied and was hired. Resurrected pride pushed aside my insecurities, and I boldly resumed my promiscuous lifestyle.

Along with the new job came new acquaintances —Diane for one, an attractive psychology major who worked in my department. We connected immediately. But increased marijuana use and heavier dependence upon the music and lyrics that shaped my thoughts took first place. Slowly, pride began to overrule any thoughts of a god other than myself. For me, the position of Supreme Being became a lofty goal, attainable for anyone bold enough to reach for it, and I'd become bold enough. My sights were brazen: to snatch the title "God."

As that journey began so did a series of coincidences: a wish fulfilled, a desire realized, a passion satisfied—each a confirmation, legitimizing my quest. Then there was the horoscope with its strange and alluring predictions. Religiously I sought direction through the stars, leaning hard in any direction

Joe Colaizzi with niece Beth before he met Christ as Savior

to ensure the outcome of my day would line up with astral projections.

Daily I grew more determined to be the one in charge and more convinced I could, until that fateful evening Diane and I decided to get high after dinner.

"Wow!" she exclaimed, exhaling the hypnotic smoke.

"What's up?" I asked.

"I just had a wicked thought."

"What was it?"

"Oh, nothing, really."

"Come on. Don't leave me hangin'. Tell me."

"I can't."

"Sure you can. You've got to."

"Well, I . . . I just saw you as Satan," she finally admitted.

Ha! I thought, *if she only knew. She's got it backwards*. But a seed had been planted in my mind.

Strangely, during the next few weeks getting high led only to depression. Both the music and coincidental happenings that had encouraged my hunger for supremacy began to turn sour. Friends disappeared; family seemed distant, almost wary of me. Dad even commented, "You have an evil look in your eyes."

Thoughts of Satan crowded my mind daily, haunting me, demanding attention, becoming harder and harder to dismiss. My plan to become "The Almighty" was now growing dim as I found myself in an emotionally charged spiritual battle for identity, which I didn't have a clue how to fight.

What's happening to me? I thought, smoking another joint. *Who am I? What am I? What's goin' on? How did I loose control—or did I?*

Answers came during a weekend visit with my folks. As I settled into Mom's favorite chair with the newspaper, the cover of the magazine insert stunned me with that alarming headline, "Satan Is Alive and Well—Living Among Us." The related article convinced me—Joe Colaizzi was Satan!

Devastated, I sat dazed, unable to move or think. When Mom entered the room, the spell was broken. I rose and moved across the room. Claiming her chair, she shot a glance toward me and said, "My, this seat is hot!"

What did you expect? I thought. *Satan just got out of it.*

Then like a flood came staggering thoughts of

lessons learned in elementary school, thoughts of Lucifer, rebellious angel, cast forever from heaven to become Satan.

The following days brought pain beyond my comprehension. Trapped inside myself I could not find escape. My last two friends, music and marijuana, had betrayed me. Strength oozed away; weakness took control. Hopeless, I wanted to scream, but a cry for help would only validate what I already knew to be true. I had committed the unpardonable sin!

▦ ▦ ▦ ▦ ▦ ▦

Locked inside this prison of hopelessness and fear, I knew the only way out was final, the consequences everlasting.

▦ ▦ ▦ ▦ ▦ ▦

Empty and alone, unable to share my impossible predicament, I wanted to—needed to—end it all. There seemed no other way. Suicide!

For weeks I considered several methods: pills, drugs, a bridge, a building. The thoughts obsessed me day and night. Sound sleep would not come; deeper depression did. The psychiatrist offered ineffective medication. I longed to die, to disappear, aching to escape from this nightmare. Locked inside a prison of hopelessness and fear, I knew the only way out was final, the consequences everlasting.

But I couldn't bring myself to do it. A lack of

courage? Fear? It didn't matter. I just knew I couldn't do it.

Seeking solace, I arrived at Diane's apartment depressed and confused. I hadn't seen her for months. She was surprised but seemed pleased to see me. Conversation moved quickly from trivialities to a sketchy description of what was happening in my mind. After only minutes Diane asked, "Joe, will you do me a favor?"

"Yeah, what?"

"Come with me. Let some people pray for you."

Yeah, right! Pray for Satan! That makes a lot of sense, I thought. *And who are you to be talkin' about prayer anyway?* "Forget it!" I said, casting a don't-be-ridiculous look at Diane.

As she persisted I began to notice something different about her. I hadn't seen this side of her before. Suddenly it hit: *Diane's got religion.* To get her off the subject, I agreed. "OK, if they can see me tonight, I'll do it."

Elated, she called her friends. Just as I'd hoped, they were unavailable. I was off the hook. Undaunted, Diane set up a meeting for the following evening.

The whole idea was insane. There was no hope for Satan. I had no intention of showing up. Yet, I did.

Diane introduced me to Dick, his wife, and Michael. As Michael's eyes met mine, I saw a radiant glow. He flinched at the evil he saw in mine.

Feeling rejected, defeated, resentful, I followed them upstairs. Their questions centered on my life-style.

"What about drugs, Joe? Any involvement there?"

"Yeah, I smoke pot. And I've experimented with some other stuff."

"Alcohol?"

"I don't have a problem with it. It's relaxing. Helps me forget. I enjoy it."

"So, you enjoy music, women, drugs, and alcohol. Anything else to tell us?"

"Yeah, I guess I oughta tell you that . . . that I'm Satan!"

Patiently, they listened, even seemed to understand, but they would not be convinced.

"Joe, you belong to Jesus," they insisted. "The devil's gotten into your mind. He's a liar and is trying to destroy you." They supported their claims with Scriptures that to me were meaningless. Yet they continued.

"Satan's trying to deceive you. But you must not believe him. Look, when you drifted away from God, any spiritual foundation you may have had crumbled. Now, you have no spiritual defense. When you smoke pot, you totally open yourself to any evil spirit that may be drifting around looking for a home, and the spirit of pride moves in, then anger, hatred, doubt, fear, depression, suicide, and so on."

Their words made sense. I only wished I could believe.

"The Lord can and will deliver you," they insisted. They read several accounts of Jesus healing people possessed by demons. But for me, hearing was one thing, believing almost impossible.

"Joe, God has given us, His followers, authority in the name of Jesus Christ, to cast these evil spirits from you."

Again they supported their claims with Scripture. Again I wanted to believe. Again it was not possible.

"We'd like to pray for you," Dick said.

Indifference and sarcasm flavored my response. "Go ahead. Pray."

Unfazed by my attitude they began. "In the name of Jesus, we bind you, Satan." With apparent authority and conviction they prayed. First Michael, next Dick, then the ladies. They addressed each spirit individually: doubt, fear, anger, hatred, depression, suicide. Embarrassed for them, I listened uncomfortably. To me the whole exercise was ridiculous, clearly a futile effort driven by the immature fantasies of these well-meaning but misdirected people. I wasn't impressed. I just wanted to take Diane home, get high, and forget the whole thing.

But Michael seemed to know my thoughts. When they ran out of demons to pray about, he looked at me and said, "Before you leave, is there anything else bothering you?"

For weeks I'd been experiencing deep pain in my upper back and neck. The pressure was intense, but, fearing surgery, I wouldn't see a doctor. Daily the pressure increased. Straightening my back was painful; my knees had no strength. Not wanting to reveal weakness, I had not told anyone. But now I figured, *Why not?*

"Yeah, there's something else bothering me."

"What is it?"

Searching for words to describe my condition, I realized that, so far, these people had addressed only intangibles—emotional, psychological, spiritual kinds of things. This was a physical problem; my attitude revealed my skepticism. *Show me your Jesus Christ this time, pal,* I thought. *Let's see what He can do with this.*

"What is it?" Michael repeated.

Still searching for words, I motioned toward my shoulder. "Well, I've got this, uh . . ."

"A yoke?" Michael offered.

I was shocked. "Yeah, that's it!"

Michael described it perfectly. "A deep pain, intense pressure, a heavy weight." He had my undivided attention.

"Jesus Christ can heal you," Michael said.

Again my attitude turned cynical. *Oh, come on!*

Whether Michael could read me this time or not, he continued with words from his Bible: "Are any among you sick? They should call for the elders of the church and have them pray over them, anointing them with oil in the name of the Lord. The prayer of faith will save the sick, and the Lord will raise them up; and anyone who has committed sins will be forgiven" (James 5:14-15, NRSV).

"Yeah, that sounds great!" I admitted out loud. But in my heart, *Those are just words in a book, man. They're nonsense!*

"Joe," Michael asked, "do you believe Jesus Christ is the Son of God?"

Catholic upbringing made the answer easy. "Yeah."

"Do you believe Jesus can heal you?"

"If He's the Son of God," I said, "I guess He can

do whatever He chooses." But I thought, *I don't believe He will.*

"Do you want to be healed?"

"Of course!"

Turning to Dick, Michael asked, "Did you bring your oil?" Reaching into his pocket, Dick withdrew a small bottle. I started looking for the door.

Taking the bottle, Michael walked over and stood beside my chair. Dick stood behind me and laid his hands on my aching shoulders. The two ladies sat quietly. With a drop of oil on his finger, Michael pressed the sign of the cross onto my forehead and ordered, "In the name of Jesus Christ, I command the spirit of oppression to leave this man and never return." Dick repeated the command. Then both men said it together. Eventually, the ladies joined in.

With confident authority they repeated the words several times, the atmosphere growing more intense with each repetition. The battle was on. Something was happening, something important. Their words were strong, not loud or boisterous, yet spoken with power and conviction.

Michael looked at me, "OK, Joe, now *you* tell that demon to leave."

I froze in silence, unsure. My thoughts raced. *They're making a fool of me. This is ridiculous.* I wanted to run.

Then, a fresh thought, *You've tried everything else. Give God a chance.* But another thought barged in. *They'll laugh at you. Don't give in.*

The battle raged within me. Confused, I struggled, hesitant to make a choice. I could feel the pain. I remembered the failed attempts to overcome depression, to escape from this insanity, the psychiatrist, the pills, the frustrated efforts of family and friends. Nothing had worked or helped.

What if these people are right? I thought. And then, *This is foolishness. Don't weaken. You'll regret it.*

Back and forth I waffled. Finally I relented. *OK, let's just see what happens.*

"In the name of Jesus, I command the spirit of oppression to leave me and never return." The fact I'd said the words surprised me. But the power and authority that seemed to flow through me as I said them surprised me even more. I felt I was in charge; yet, I knew it was so much more than me.

■ ■ ■ ■ ■ ■

"It's gone! The weight, the pain, they're gone!"

■ ■ ■ ■ ■ ■

Silence followed. Michael turned and walked quietly to his chair. Dick lifted his hands from my shoulders.

"Wha . . . what happened?" I exclaimed turning toward Dick. "What did you do?"

"Nothing. Why?"

"It's gone! The weight, the pain, they're gone!"

"Jesus Christ has healed you, Joe," he said, beaming.

"I've gotta stand up," I announced, testing my

21

knees for strength. The weakness had vanished. I couldn't believe the change. My entire body felt restored. I smiled for the first time in months. *Unbelievable!* I thought. *Maybe there's some truth to this Jesus stuff.*

Free at last, I was ready to celebrate. With thoughts of getting high, I gave Diane a let's-go-party look, grabbed my jacket, took her arm, and moved toward the door.

Michael stopped me with his words. "One more thing before you leave."

"Yeah, what's that?"

"Jesus cautions that when an evil spirit leaves a man, it will seek another place to rest. Finding none, it will return to the one it left, bringing with it seven spirits more wicked than itself."

I was angry. "Great! So, what do I do now?"

Calmly, gently, Michael explained. "You need to build a spiritual foundation."

"Yeah, and how do I do that?"

"You need to open your heart and life to Jesus. Build a personal relationship with Him. Get to know Him. Read His Word. Pray. Get involved in a church where other believers meet. And you need to tell somebody what the Lord has done for you."

Not what I wanted to hear. I'd worked hard to avoid things like these—things that would reveal weakness and tarnish my macho self-made-man image. "Christian" was not the image I wanted to portray.

With mixed emotions, I left with Diane, dropped her off at her apartment, and returned to my own.

2
Noah's Ark

For quite some time I sat alone, thinking, wondering. *What will the future hold? Can I turn my back on my past? Do I want to? Can I maintain my image and still check out this Jesus?* At last I gave in. *OK, Jesus, You're on. Let's see what You can do.* Haughty? Perhaps, but rooted in a sincere hope.

Old habits were hard to break. Confusion came easy. Decisions were difficult. Michael and the prayer team hooked me up with a pastor who patiently counseled and mentored me. Still, Bible reading was a struggle—I found an old Catholic version buried in the closet—and church attendance intimidating. But I was determined to honor my commitment—at least for a little while. Prayers were awkward and sporadic. Answers seemed to come, but I was hard to convince.

Several months into the journey, I became frustrated and upset. Alone in my apartment, I cried out, "Jesus, I need help. I'm struggling. My life's still a mess. Everywhere I turn I'm reminded of my past. I need to get away. But where should I go? How would I get there? You tell me, Jesus. And, if You're really God, so I'll know it's from You, tell me through Dolly." An impossible condition—I hadn't seen her for years. To expect this woman, the wife I had betrayed, to contact me was unreasonable. I almost wished I hadn't made the request.

23

In frustration I wept. "Lord, I feel like such a failure! I can't even make a simple decision, and I have nowhere else to turn."

I poured out my heart. Silence. Had He heard? Did He care? Was He as disgusted with me as I was with myself? What would be next?

The knock on the apartment door startled me. Quickly, I straightened up my appearance and opened the door. I was dumbfounded, speechless—it was Dolly!

"Joe C, aren't you going to invite me in?"

"Dolly!" I finally managed, "Uh . . . sure . . . sorry. Come on in. What are you doing here?"

Smiling, she stepped into the room. Following a few awkward pleasantries, I offered her a seat.

"Joe C, know what you ought to do?"

"No. What?"

"Take my Volkswagen van and go to Santa Fe, New Mexico. Right now. Tonight."

I was stunned. It hadn't been five minutes since I'd asked God for the impossible, and here sat Dolly with the answer. No longer could I doubt. I would follow Jesus.

■ ■ ■

Three days, maybe four—life was such a blur— and I showed up in Santa Fe. Annie, a pretty little friend of Dolly's who was barely surviving as a construction worker, welcomed me with open arms. I felt awkward.

"How's Dolly? What brings you here? How long can you stay?"

Questions came faster than answers. I was unsure, unconnected, uncomfortable, still working through the lingering effects of marijuana in my brain. I gave Annie the stereo Dolly had asked me to deliver, which seemed to be the only reason I'd even made the trip. She offered to put me up for the night. I accepted. She fed me dinner, and I collapsed.

Morning came quickly and with it about an hour of Bible reading and prayer, a routine I could never have imagined, but one that was fast becoming a staple since this adventure with Jesus began.

Annie offered breakfast. I was grateful but not much company. Afterward I thanked her and announced, "I'm leaving."

"Where're you going?"

"Back home."

"You just got here."

"Yeah, but I need to get back to my job and all."

Unsure of myself, I waved good-bye to a puzzled Annie and headed east.

■ ■ ■ ■ ■ ■

I zigzagged back and forth across America, confused but determined to find the Lord's will.

■ ■ ■ ■ ■ ■

Second-guessing my decision from the start, I stopped several hundred miles later to pray for direction. The brightly painted letters on the side of the westbound semitrailer spelled "Safeway." That seemed to be my answer—for the moment. So westbound I went, back toward Santa Fe. But conflicting thoughts raced through my mind. *This can't be right. It must be. I have responsibilities in Pittsburgh. But God directed me, or did He?"*

Back and forth I went, in my mind and on the road. Hundreds of miles east, then west, frantically seeking direction, never convinced I'd received it.

As hours turned into days and days into weeks, I zigzagged back and forth across America, confused but determined to find the Lord's will.

Nearly three weeks into the journey, my 7:00 A.M. devotional time led to the story of Noah and the flood. I'd heard it all before. This was getting me nowhere. "Lord," I cried, "I need an answer. If You want me in Santa Fe, tell me. Somehow give me a clear sign, something unmistakably from You."

Frustrated, I wept at length.

With fresh resolve, I continued my indecisive path, east and west, wanting to obey, hoping to learn how, my infant faith struggling to grow.

About midnight the rain began as I headed east on Interstate 70. Visibility quickly decreased as the rain intensified. Humidity rose inside the van. The inefficient defroster offered little help. Soon cars, pickups, even semitrailers, had pulled over to wait out the storm.

The next thoughts scared me. *The story of Noah and the flood was a warning. The stubborn and disobedient perished. I've had my chances. God is upset. My time is up.*

Frightened and disoriented, I strained, looking for the next exit. Unable to see clearly, I pulled into what appeared to be a large parking lot. Climbing into the back of the van, discouraged with my inability to understand the Lord's direction, I curled up and prayed myself to sleep.

The bright morning sun woke me early. Uncertain I was even still alive, I rose slowly to my knees. Peering through the narrow window of the van's sliding door, I stared in disbelief. There stood Noah! Poised on the deck of a huge ark-shaped structure was a larger-than-life sized statue of a man surrounded by animals. A dove was perched on a finger of his outstretched arm.

The sign read Noah's Ark Motor Hotel. To me it said: "I hear your prayers. This is your answer. Go to Santa Fe. Trust Me. I love you."

Joe with his VW van in front of Noah's Ark Motor Hotel

3
Boot Camp

Annie was surprised when I returned, but gracious nonetheless. She put me up for a couple of weeks and put up with me as I continued to struggle with indecision. Learning that Annie expected other company, I knew I had to leave.

Again I was thinking Pittsburgh. Annie suggested Bourbon and Blues, a local nightclub we'd visited the week before. "You never know who you'll meet there," she said. "Never know what'll happen."

Frankly, I wasn't interested. I thanked her and took off, certain I should return to my job at the university. But it was late, and I was tired.

Why I pulled into the nightclub parking lot was a mystery to me. Finding myself sitting at the bar was even more puzzling. I ordered a Coke. As if by divine appointment I heard, "Hey, how ya doin', man. Weren't ya here last week? Yeah, I danced with your girl, right?"

Bob was an outgoing, easy-to-like guy. We talked for some time. I told him about the Lord and how He'd been dealing with me, about Annie, and my plans to return to Pittsburgh. "Hey, you don't have to leave," he offered. "You can stay at my place."

His place was a shabby, single-car garage. I got the couch. Bob worked in the historic section of Santa Fe at a jewelry store inside the Santa Fe Vil-

Joe in front of the Santa Fe Village in
Santa Fe, New Mexico

lage, an adobe shopping center several miles from
the apartment. He had no transportation, so I earned
my keep shuffling him back and forth. We survived
on fried onions, potatoes, and oatmeal. It didn't matter though, because during my morning devotions
somewhere between Pittsburgh and Santa Fe, between Proverbs 3 and Matthew 6, I'd made another
commitment: I would trust the Lord completely and
make His priorities mine. If I understood what I'd
been reading, He would surely direct me and meet
my basic needs. As a result, my faith should grow. So
far, so good.

■ ■ ■

Six weeks after leaving Pittsburgh, I was close to broke. Waiting for Bob one evening just outside the shop I prayed: *Lord, I'm down to my last few bucks, just enough to buy gas to get home. If a door doesn't open to stay in Santa Fe, I'll take it that You want me in Pittsburgh.*

Only minutes passed. "Hey, Joe." It was Roberto, an enthusiastic young Mexican-American whom I'd met days earlier at the Christian bookstore, a few doors from the silver shop. Roberto was a regular at the shopping center. He washed dishes at the restaurant there.

"Eef you want a job, Joe, you can geet one washeen deeshes at dee restaurant."

I applied. The Santa Fe Creperie Restaurant was owned by a kind man with a pleasantly disarming smile and a generous spirit. He introduced himself as Nick. During a brief interview I learned he also owned the Christian bookstore. He offered me the job along with an invitation to his Tuesday night Bible study. I accepted both. "If you need a place to stay," he said, "you can stay upstairs. Use the night watchman's bed while he's on duty."

"Thanks, but I have a place."

"Well, just know you're welcome."

Two days later Bob informed me that his landlady had requested my departure, and my faith continued to grow. "Your Father knows what you need before you ask him" (Matt. 6:8*b*).

Clearly the Lord was not finished with me in

Santa Fe. So, I called my boss at the university and explained I wasn't ready to return.

"How will you know when you're ready?" he asked.

"The Lord will tell me," I explained, expecting a laugh. Surprisingly, he seemed to understand. He arranged a leave of absence for me, guaranteeing my job for a year. That arrangement released me to concentrate on my relationship with Jesus and this adventure of faith in Santa Fe.

In a seven-month period, washing dishes led to assistant cook and eventually restaurant manager. Sleep was often sacrificed. Days were spent working; nights, in the Word. Roberto's gift, a brand-new KJV Bible helped. Faith-building lessons came daily. The Lord revealed pride, stretched patience, increased trust, removed habits, answered prayer, met needs, gave direction, healed hurts, and brought comfort, peace, and joy. Talk about a "new creature," He was certainly working on me.

■ ■ ■ ■ ■ ■

But no matter what,
I was determined to trust God
for my food. Always.
Well, not exactly always.

■ ■ ■ ■ ■ ■

Payday was usually an interesting experience. I was convinced that accepting money would somehow short-circuit my dependence on God and restrict my growth in faith. Nick disagreed. He insisted on paying me. I refused. The debate went on.

Food was also an issue. Nick had said when he hired me, "Help yourself to anything you want to eat." Though grateful, I had already decided to turn my diet over to God. I'd wait on Him to send someone with an invitation whenever He wanted me to eat. Every day was different. Maybe I'd eat, maybe I wouldn't. Some days a glass of water was offered; on occasion, steak and eggs. But no matter what, I was determined to trust God for my food. Always. Well, not exactly always. There were those early morning raids on blueberry pie and ice cream, a few peanut butter sandwiches, and maybe a soda every once in awhile. But for the most part, with the Lord's help, I kept my commitment.

Another challenge was clothing. The soles of my boots had worn thin. It was tempting and would have been easy to ask Nick for a few bucks to buy a new pair, but I refused. I'd wait on God. When I left Pittsburgh I had no idea I'd be away this long. So I hadn't brought much with me—a couple changes of clothes, the boots I was wearing, my Bible, and a guitar. I'd almost forgotten the guitar. I'd hidden it in the back of the van. A few months into the journey, remembering I'd brought it, I decided to play, only to discover the guitar had been stolen. Disappointed? Extremely! But angry with God better describes my feelings. How could He have let this happen? I was trusting Him, wasn't I? And He'd let me down. Eventually, however, I began to accept the loss.

Word about the stolen guitar spread quickly around the shopping center. One evening, a rather powerfully built Mexican entered the restaurant, carrying a guitar. He was looking for me. His dark eyes and radiant face were sharply framed by long black hair and almost hidden behind a full black beard. He introduced himself as Ramon. He'd been to the bookstore to post an ad for the guitar he was selling, and the clerk sent him to see me. I examined the instrument, played it, and liked it.

"How much do you want?" I asked.

"Feefty dollars. But eef you buy thees geetar, you must promise to take very good care of eet."

"Certainly I'd take good care of it. But why would you ask me to promise that?"

"Because thees geetar came to me een a very special way."

"Oh yeah, and how was that?"

Flashing a piercing stare into my eyes, he said strongly, "The Lord Jesus Christ gave me thees geetar."

His words stimulated my desire to own the instrument, but I was broke. I asked Ramon if he'd return on Friday night for an answer after I prayed about it. He agreed. My prayer was simple and straightforward. "Lord, you know my situation, my desires, my needs. If it's Your will for me to have that guitar, please make a way."

The following afternoon as I prepared for dinner, Nick's son-in-law, Ronnie, who managed a silver shop near the restaurant, wandered into the kitchen as he often did. "Joe, you look troubled," he said. "What's on your mind?"

"Oh, nothin' much. Just prayin'."

"Anything serious?"

"Not really, just prayin' about a guitar I saw."

"Oh, I didn't know you played."

"Actually, I just like to mess around on it."

■ ■ ■ ■ ■ ■

I proudly handed him the $50 and accepted the guitar that the Lord was now giving to me.

■ ■ ■ ■ ■ ■

"Well, what is it Joe? You need money? How much are they asking?"

"Fifty bucks."

"Well," he said, pulling a roll of bills from his pocket, "here ya go." He peeled off two 20s and a 10, slapped them on the counter, and disappeared.

Friday night when Ramon returned, I proudly handed him the $50 and accepted the guitar that the Lord was now giving to me. Curious, I asked Ramon why he was selling it.

"I'm movin' to the hills," he explained, "and need money to buy supplies." After selling his possessions, he planned to drop into Mexico, buy a bunch of trinkets, and sell them in the States. With the profit he'd buy needed supplies for his move to the hills outside Santa Fe. We chatted for a few moments more, and Ramon was gone.

For the next few weeks, it was business as usual,

and I enjoyed my new guitar. But my boots were becoming more of a problem. This became painfully clear in the gravel parking lot outside the restaurant when a sharp rock sliced through the sole of one boot. Quickly, I reminded the Lord of my need. My dependence upon Him had become a bit of a joke among the non-Christians at the restaurant, and they seemed to be enjoying my current dilemma. But I was determined to trust—and wait.

It was a complete surprise when Ramon returned several weeks later. I thought I'd never see the man again, but here he stood with a brown paper sack crumpled under his arm.

"Hey, Ramon!" I exclaimed, excited to see him. "You make it to Mexico?"

"Yeah," was his curt reply.

"Well, how'd it go?"

"Pretty good."

"You find what you were lookin' for?"

"Yeah."

"Well, what'd you bring back?" I asked, trying to stimulate conversation.

"Leetle beet o' thees an' a leetle beet o' that."

"Hey, what's in the bag? Something you brought back with you?"

"Yeah."

"Let's see what ya got."

He handed me the bag. The contents took my breath away—a pair of made-in-Mexico shoes, exactly my size. This stranger could not have known my need. Someone handed Ramon 20 bucks, and the shoes were mine.

Every answered prayer strengthened my faith. But the impact began to reach far beyond me. Many of the shopping center employees, Christians and non-Christians alike, were amazed as they witnessed God meet even the simplest of needs.

Ramon and I soon became good friends. I'd often drive him to the hills on weekends and help prepare his new place for his eventual move.

■ ■ ■

Life had changed radically for me since that night with Michael and the prayer team a few short months earlier. The Lord had taken the shattered pieces of my broken life and was shaping them into something completely new and exciting. Now I was free. I'd been forgiven. I had faith. I had hope. I had peace. I had Him.

Ready for the future, I began to pray for direction.

■ ■ ■

It was about mid-May when Dolly called. "Joe C, can you pick me up?"

"Well, ah . . . sure. Where are you?"

"I just flew in to Albuquerque."

As we drove from the airport to Santa Fe, Dolly asked if I'd drive her to Pittsburgh. Perhaps that was my direction. I prayed for confirmation.

When I dropped her off at the motel in Santa Fe, she asked me to wait while she called her father. When they finished talking, he asked for me. "When ya comin' home, son?" he asked. He said his son Joe, the youngest of Dolly's three brothers, was starting a construction company and could use my help.

That sealed it for me. I wrapped things up with Nick at the restaurant. With his blessing and a sense of release, I took off for Pittsburgh with Dolly.

Seven months in Santa Fe had been an education. Faithful to His Word, God had met my needs and was clearly directing my path. He'd been growing my faith and teaching me to trust, building the spiritual foundation Michael had suggested the night the Lord delivered me.

4
The Worker Is Worth His Keep

In Pittsburgh the adventure continued. Ron, another of Dolly's brothers, provided housing while I worked with Joe as he tried to get his new construction company off the ground. I had no interest in returning to the university. Life was different now, and so was I. As the months unfolded, Ron accepted the Lord. Through his witness Dolly also opened her heart.

Dolly's sister, Barbara, had been ill for years. At Dolly's request, the three of us went expectantly to hear faith healer Kathryn Khulman speak in downtown Pittsburgh. Although our hope for Barbara's healing went unfulfilled, I felt I'd found a church home.

Joe's hopes for his new carpenter went unfulfilled also. My tendency toward perfectionism probably cost him more time, money, and frustration than anyone cared to admit. Graciously he put up with me for about a year and a half. Eventually I left the company and picked up a few odd jobs around town.

When Ron's house went up for sale, my parents invited me home—with one condition: "No preaching." They were struggling with my new "religion" and required me to keep it to myself. We had our awkward moments.

The garage Joe and his father built together

Several months into my stay, Dad expressed a concern that the garage behind his house seemed unsafe. After careful examination we agreed the garage must come down. Dad and I would build a new one, the fulfillment of desire that had burned in my heart since childhood: to work with Dad on an important project and maybe get to know him better. Also, this might provide an opportunity to share my faith with him.

Together we designed it. Throughout the summer we worked, building his garage and our relationship. Although it would be several years before he'd receive the Lord, Dad clearly saw and openly acknowledged His intervention throughout the building process. As our project drew toward completion, I began again to sense the need for further direction.

■ ■ ■ ■ ■ ■

"Here I am, Lord.
No strings attached."

■ ■ ■ ■ ■ ■

Sunday morning services for the Kathryn Khulman ministry were held in Youngstown, Ohio. The
70-mile drive offered plenty of time to pray. Powerful answers came through the sermons. That was the
case the morning Moishe Rosen, founder and then
executive director of the Jews for Jesus organization,
preached. He spoke of the radical obedience and to-
tal commitment of Abraham and Paul and about the
great spiritual need and the tremendous possibilities
in New York City. Thousands, he said, could be
reached in only hours by handing out tracts in
Grand Central Station. His challenge? Make our-
selves completely available to God, totally obedient,
no strings attached.

Touching spiritual nerves deep within my heart,
the message moved me to earnestly pledge, "Here I
am, Lord. No strings attached."

For days I thought a lot about that message and
my commitment. The longer I thought about it the
more convinced I became—the Lord wanted me to
go to New York City, probably the only place on the
planet I did *not* want to go.

I'd been there once, years before with some
friends. I remembered a cold, impersonal, intimidating town. I didn't like New York. Perhaps a waiter

had something to do with that. I had ordered breakfast at Ham 'N' Eggs, a fast-food restaurant in midtown Manhattan. After an extremely long wait, the food finally arrived, but not what I had ordered. Hungry and in a hurry, I ate my fill and decided that, for such poor service, there would be no tip. Stepping out onto the busy sidewalk, I was absorbed into a multitude of people. Vehicles of all descriptions crowded the streets. Blasting horns and screaming sirens competed with a cacophony of other unrecognizable, irritating sounds.

As I crossed a busy intersection, a vaguely familiar voice screamed above the noise, "It's customary in New York to tip when we're served!" It was my waiter. Shocked and embarrassed, I flipped him a coin and disappeared into the crowd.

I did *not* want to go to New York City. But I couldn't shake the conviction—New York was exactly where the Lord wanted me.

Weeks of denial and stubborn resistance finally ended in surrender. I accepted the challenge. But how would I travel? Where would I stay? What would I do in NYC?

Matthew chapter 10 had some answers. Preach the Word, love people, and keep trusting. Take no money, no change of clothes, no extra shoes. Simply trust Him for everything, because "the worker is worth his keep" (Matt. 10:10*b*). The whole thing seemed ludicrous, but in my heart I knew it was the Lord.

Discreetly over the next few days, I gave my tools away and signed my car over to Dolly. With only my Bible and guitar, I slipped quietly out of my folks' house; they'd never understand this move. I spent my last night in Pittsburgh with Dolly and her father, Babe. She would drop me off at the turnpike in the morning. I would hitchhike to New York.

Another adventure of faith.

5
Use Wisdom, Son

I rose early the next morning. I needed to pray. Nip, the family dog, followed me out to the dew-covered field. "One last time, Lord, I need confirmation here. This is a pretty crazy expedition I'm contemplating, and if it isn't from You, I'd sure like a door to close. If it is from You, I need some kind of a sign."

"Joe C, come get some breakfast." It was Babe. As Dolly and I ate, Babe was busy in another room. After breakfast he called me in. "Well, whacha think?" he asked. "Will this help?" His artwork on the table spoke volumes. On a legal-size file folder he'd printed in huge letters the words "New York." To Babe it was a sign for hitchhiking. To me it was a sign from the Lord.

Energized by this answer, I gathered up my Bible and guitar, tucked the sign under my arm, and headed for the door. Babe stopped me. "Here, son, you're gonna need this," he offered, pressing a five-dollar bill into my hand.

"Thanks," I said with grateful surprise, and off I went with Dolly to the turnpike where we said good-bye. As she drove away, I stood there on faith alone, waiting, hoping, trusting.

Minutes turned slowly into an hour. I was becoming restless. Neither the sign nor my thumb had drawn even the slightest interest. Again the ques-

Joe's "New York" sign—a sign from the Lord

tions came: *If this is from You, Lord, where's my ride? I mean, You're God. You can certainly provide one. I figured You would have had this thing worked out more precisely.*

At that point a thought crossed my mind. *Do you trust Me?* It was the Lord.

Do I trust You? Ha! Look at me? Look at my life, what I'm doing, where I've been. Do I trust *You? Lord, You* know *I trust You.*

If you trust Me, came the next thought, *you don't need that five-dollar bill.* Of all the . . . ! I couldn't believe it. But then, I *could.* If I trusted Him completely, I needed only Him.

So, standing on the eastbound side of the Pennsylvania Turnpike on that wind-whipped October morning, I pulled the five from my pocket, crumpled it into a ball, and tossed it blindly over my shoulder into the bushes behind.

It seemed only an instant later that a car pulled over. "Hey, Joe. Where ya headed?" It was Eric, a young man I'd recently met playing football. He was traveling east with a friend. For the next 50 miles we talked about Jesus. The adventure had begun.

And so it went all the way to New York—sports cars to semitrailers, individuals to families, one ride after another, all interested in my adventure and the Lord who was behind it.

A young couple provided my last ride for the day. They offered me food as we drove, but I declined. I needed to be extra sensitive to the Lord's voice. I wasn't eating.

Just after midnight they dropped me off on the New Jersey side of the George Washington Bridge, just across the Hudson River from Manhattan. Hitch-hiking on the bridge was illegal, according to the sign, so I began to walk across the massive structure, eight lanes above and another six lanes below. Traffic was heavy even at that late hour. The brisk wind pushed against me, stinging my face. Still I paused midway across, drinking in the beauty of the scene—New York City standing proudly, just a stone's throw away, radiantly aglow, sharply outlined against a black eastern sky.

As traffic noise from the bridge and the river below competed with my thoughts, adrenaline pumped as never before, and I screamed loudly for only God and me to hear, "Are you ready for me, New York City?" I was excited. I had no clue what the future held, but I knew the One who did, and He was holding my hand.

I exited the bridge, climbed the grassy embankment, and stopped to get my bearings. "Amsterdam Ave. and 178th St." the sign read, quite a distance from 42nd Street where the Jews for Jesus office was located. For whatever reason, I was convinced I needed to find that office. Hoping for a shortcut, I sought directions.

The fast-food shop on the corner was empty, but the door was unlocked. The drab gray walls were bare. A thick, transparent glass wall reached high above the countertop.

"Anyone home?" I hollered.

Through a doorway behind the glass a large black man appeared and ambled toward me. Reaching the counter, he rested his hands against it and leaned in my direction. "Yeah," his deep voice commanded, "whachoo want, boy?"

"Well, I need to get to 42nd Street, and I thought you might be able to direct me."

Graciously he explained, but his directions assumed I had a vehicle. When he finished I asked, "How would I get there walkin'?"

■ ■ ■ ■ ■ ■

"Boy, if you walk there tonight, you gonna git killed."

■ ■ ■ ■ ■ ■

"You cain't walk there tonight, boy!"

"Pardon me?"

"I said you cain't walk there tonight."

"Why not?"

"You'll git yoself killed!"

"I don't understand."

"Boy, if you walk there tonight, you gonna git *killed*. You gonna git shot or stabbed. Somethin' bad's gonna happen t' ya."

I wasn't worried. "Man, I've got Jesus Christ with me," I announced with confidence.

Leaning closer, he leveled his stare, carefully measuring his next words. "I don't care who ya got witchoo, boy. You cain't walk there tonight! You gonna git killed!"

With pride and naïveté I thanked him and left. Strolling out into the cold dark night, I thought, *Lord, if he only knew how much I trust You.*

A stronger, sobering thought stormed into my mind. *Use wisdom, son.* It was the Lord.

Then it hit. My life *was* at risk. I was a stranger, lost in the dark streets of an unfamiliar city and had just been warned by a local merchant. Cautiously I looked around. Trash, dominated by wine jugs, beer cans, and whisky bottles, littered the landscape. I was

136 blocks from my destination, and I was the only white person in the neighborhood.

Wisdom said "pray." Promptly I obeyed. *Lord, please protect and guide me.*

Almost instantly an old black man popped out of the shadows. His heavy overcoat, several sizes too large and frayed at the hem, reeked of filth. The collar and sleeves were stained and worn. Buttons were missing, but not missed. His dirty, unshaven face hid behind a mostly gray, unkempt beard. His sweat-stained hat was wrinkled and worn. He smelled of body odor, urine, and cheap wine. Expectantly he reached an upturned palm toward me, "Ya got a quarter fo' somethin' ta drink, man?"

"Sorry, bro, I don't have any money. But I'll share what I have with you."

"Yeah? Whachoo got, man?"

"Jesus Christ," I said.

"Jesus Christ! Whazzat, man?"

Herbie was hungry for the Good News. The more he heard, the more he wanted to hear. With amazing interest and understanding, he fired question after question. Herbie wanted to learn about Jesus. Through the streets we walked, instant best friends—Herbie and me, "partners" for the night.

He'd forgotten about the drink but was determined to find a cigarette. I tried hard to convince him that Jesus could deliver him from the habit, but Herbie was resolute. When he wasn't searching the ground for discarded butts, he was stopping anyone he saw—cab drivers, pedestrians, bus drivers, you name it. Herbie craved a cigarette.

Eventually, a young black man approached, smoking. Herbie ran to meet him. His appetite finally satisfied, Herbie walked with the young man toward me. That's when I noticed the tears.

■ ■ ■ ■ ■ ■

With the help of Herbie's amen-brother punctuation, I attempted to assure Jo Jo that Jesus could help him and his wife.

■ ■ ■ ■ ■ ■

Jo Jo, our new friend, wept uncontrollably as he shared his story. He'd been singing in a local bar and flirting with a strange woman when his wife walked in. She exploded. He tried to explain. She wouldn't listen. Viciously she lashed out, hitting him repeatedly, screaming, threatening divorce. Jo Jo hit her back and ran. His life had just come crashing down. Hopelessly he'd been roaming the streets, considering suicide. He simply didn't care anymore.

When Jo Jo finished, Herbie took charge, boldly announcing, "Man, dat ain't nothin' fo' Jesus ta fix. Tell em, man!" he demanded, looking at me. "Tell em 'bout Jesus."

With the help of Herbie's amen-brother punctuation, I attempted to assure Jo Jo that Jesus could help him and his wife through this difficult time, that no matter how impossible his situation seemed, the Lord was able to bring good out of it.

Hours passed. Slowly, the words began to hit their mark. Jo Jo's eyes had a spark of hope. No longer did he want to end it all. He invited Herbie and me to spend the few remaining nighttime hours at his small apartment. There we talked until dawn about salvation and the life-changing power of Jesus. Finally Jo Jo was convinced.

None of us wanted our special time to end, but we knew it had to. As I prepared to leave, Jo Jo handed me $1.00—50 cents for subway fare to 42nd Street ("the Times Square station," he said) and 50 cents spending money. He and Herbie escorted me to the subway, offering advice all the way. "Watch yo back, man. Keep yo eyes an' ears open. We'll wait witchoo till da train come. Git on a car wit lotsa people."

"Why all the fuss?" I asked.

"Dis is *Harlem*. Yo a white boy, an' it ain't safe in Harlem fo' no white boy."

Suddenly, it all made sense: the merchant's warning, the Lord's counsel to use wisdom, Herbie's companionship, Jo Jo's concern, all from the Lord designed to protect and guide me. Had I walked to 42nd Street that night, I'd have traveled straight through Harlem, and this naive white boy with his Bible and guitar surely would have been killed. (Later I learned that even in broad daylight I wouldn't have been safe in Harlem.)

The train soon arrived, and from a crowded car I waved good-bye to my "guardian angels."

6
I Ain't Makin' No Deals

Arriving in Times Square, my first objective was to contact Jews for Jesus. I had the phone number and, thanks to Jo Jo, enough change for a few phone calls. It took three. When I finally made connection, I was invited to visit. Things would surely fall into place.

Hurrying several blocks to the building, I took the elevator to the Jews for Jesus office. With interest, the office manager listened as I recapped events since Moishe Rosen's message. "Brother Joe," I expected him to say, "welcome to New York City. We've been looking for someone just like you. Let's have dinner, then I'll show you to your room."

No such luck. After hearing my story, he affirmed my convictions and welcomed me to town. He offered some scriptural encouragement from Isaiah 43, prayed for me, then bid me farewell.

I was baffled. I'd been certain that Jews for Jesus would connect me with necessary resources in NYC. But here I stood, helplessly in need with nothing but faith.

Well, Lord, I thought, stepping back onto the sidewalk. *What's next?*

Look around, He seemed to say. *What do you see?*

Buildings, buses, taxis, people—that's what I see.
Well, there you have it. Your work is cut out for you.
Excuse me, Lord? I don't understand.
Look again, son.

And then my eyes were opened. People! Everywhere I looked, I saw people who needed to hear the Good News, and it was my job to start takin' it to the streets.

It wasn't hard to share my faith. Opportunities were everywhere: the cab driver waiting for a fare, a wandering derelict, inquisitive tourists, the homeless old woman huddled over the steam grate keeping warm, drug dealers and users on 42nd Street, the proud pimp, businessmen hurrying to and from the subway. The field was ripe for harvest, and I was a busy man.

Throughout that day and night, one encounter led to another. Some listened; others laughed; one prayed.

Proverbs 3:5-6 and Matthew 6:33 continued to fuel my faith. If I trusted and acknowledged Him, He would direct me. If my highest priorities were His interests and values, He'd meet my basic needs. Uncertain as to how or when He would do these things, I subconsciously expected the offer of a meal and a place to rest, but received none. As night turned into day and day back into night, I faithfully pursued my assignment, trusting, hoping. Soon a week had passed.

Not wanting to appear homeless or in need, I kept myself clean and clean-shaven using the rest rooms in the Port Authority bus terminal and Grand

Central Station. When the police weren't prodding the homeless to "move on," the chairs and benches in the huge waiting rooms of those facilities provided for brief periods of rest and countless unsuccessful attempts at sleep. The Catholic church on 42nd Street offered warmth and a quiet place to kneel and pray and sometimes doze off.

■ ■ ■ ■ ■ ■

"I don't really care any more, Lord," I pouted, storming into the bus terminal.

■ ■ ■ ■ ■ ■

Lacking understanding, yet certain God had called me to this task, I was determined to trust Him. But by midnight of the seventh day my body ached for food and sleep. Gradually, my focus drifted away from Jesus and onto Joe. That led to disappointment, frustration, and anger.

"I don't really care any more, Lord," I pouted, storming into the bus terminal. "I'm hungry and tired. I need rest. And the first empty chair I find, I'm claiming. I'm going to sleep." Self-righteously, I stomped through the crowded lobby, lost in myself. But the words I overheard stopped me cold. "Yeah, it's amazing! When you fast from things like food and sleep, the Lord can really use you."

Reluctantly, I retraced my last few steps and interrupted. "Excuse me, but I need to talk with you."

When the two men finished talking and one man left to catch a bus, my mentor-for-the-evening and I sat and talked. His words brought perspective. "Seek forgiveness for your rebellious attitude," he encouraged. "Pledge yourself again in service to the Lord, and trust Him to use you for His glory."

His words humbled me; his prayer brought comfort. Then we parted ways.

■ ■ ■

Refreshed, I sought direction. That led to Trevor, a young Marine who'd married his childhood sweetheart while home on a three-day pass and subsequently missed his bus. Now AWOL and certain his commanding officer (CO) hated him, Trevor feared severe punishment.

"Jesus can help," I offered.

Trevor listened closely, and 20 minutes later he opened his heart. Instantly his countenance and attitude changed. Confidently he announced, "I'll call my CO and explain. I'm sure he'll understand."

Trevor left to find a phone; I sat amazed. His heart had been prepared, and I'd have missed the chance to introduce him to the Lord had I gone my own way. The Lord had used me in spite of my rebellion. Thanking Him, I began to nod off.

When Trevor returned, he was ecstatic. "Hey, it's OK, man. My CO understood. He said to just hurry back. No penalty. Thanks, man. Thanks."

"Thank the Lord, Trevor," I said, closing my eyes for some serious sleep.

Talk to him, came the next thought.

Talk to him? Lord, I have nothing to say.
Tell him I love him.

With heavy eyes and slurred speech, I obeyed. "The Lord loves you, Trevor. And He's gonna help you get that driver's license."

Surprised by my own words, I stared at the Marine. He stared back in disbelief.

"How'd you know about the driver's license?"

"Ah . . . what driver's license?"

"*My* driver's license. I've been trying to get it for three years. And it's always something . . . failed written test . . . couldn't borrow a car for the driving test . . . flunked the driving test. I just haven't been able to get that license. How did you know?"

"I *didn't* know, Trevor, but *God* did. And I think He just used my mouth to tell you He's gonna help you get it."

That night Trevor walked away with hope, and I was recharged, ready for more.

■ ■ ■

Opportunities came often and with them encouragement. While hunger and fatigue continued to scream for attention, I knew the Lord was doing something special in my life. So I trusted, sometimes reluctantly, sometimes with great enthusiasm, trying to keep my eyes off Joe and on Jesus.

I met Harold beside the magazine stand near the subway entrance on 42nd Street. His questions searched deep, implying a serious interest in Jesus, perhaps because his life was in the process of unraveling. Recently he'd lost his job; his apartment would be next. He needed to move and asked if I'd consider helping him pack. *He* thought we could finish by morning. *I* thought I'd lead him to the Lord.

A 40-minute subway ride and a 20-minute walk got us to his apartment. There wasn't much left to do. When we finished a few hours later, he offered me a peanut butter sandwich and a place to sleep. Without prayer or hesitation, I accepted both, only to find out shortly thereafter what my friend was there after. He was gay! And I was gone.

Although his advance had fallen flat, it had shocked me, angered me. I felt betrayed, yet I was comforted knowing that Harold had heard the truth. He needed only to repent and receive. The choice was his.

Out into the darkness I went, a long distance from Times Square. I had no money to ride, but I did have an idea.

The subway was two stories below ground. Dim, random lighting cast eerie shadows on the unpainted concrete walls. The female attendant, tucked safely away in her concrete and glass booth, was the only sign of life. I placed my key-chain pocketknife on the counter in front of her and asked if she'd trade it for the 50-cent ride back to Times Square.

"Boy, I ain't makin' no deals like that!" she snapped, pushing the knife away. "I'm gonna turn my head, and if you wanna jump over that gate an' git on that train, you go right ahead, but I ain't makin' no deals like that!"

I didn't like her idea any more than she liked mine. There *had* to be another way. I retrieved the knife and moved toward the stairs considering my options.

"Lord, I'm stuck," I prayed. "It's a long hike back to Times Square." Then echoing off the bare concrete walls, the click, clack, click, of a man's footsteps grew louder.

"Hey, bro," he called. "What's up? You need a token?"

Surprised, I turned and nodded to the well-dressed black man about 30 paces away. The token he flipped through the air landed squarely in my hand. Smiling he continued on his way.

And my faith continued to increase. "And my God will meet all your needs according to his glorious riches in Christ Jesus" (Phil. 4:19).

Still, it wasn't easy. Since I'd left Pittsburgh more than a week earlier, I'd rested very little and slept even less. My ankles had swollen to twice their normal size. I'd eaten only a peanut butter sandwich and had to concentrate hard to resist the alluring fragrances of roasting chestnuts, brewing coffee, and frying bacon wafting throughout the city and beckoning me daily. Staying focused was a challenge.

7
Welcome Home

The Christian bookstore seemed strangely out of place in New York City, but I was glad to find it. I'd often wanted to leave a tract with the people I met on the streets. I introduced myself and my idea to the store manager, who was sympathetic but regretfully unable to assist. She suggested the New York Bible Society several blocks away. Then she handed me a magazine titled *Alternatives* that listed Christian ministries located throughout the metro area. She pointed out an advertisement for The Lamb's Supper Club that featured fine food and gospel entertainment.

"Maybe these folks can help you," she said. "I understand they're a group of young Christians, who recently moved into the Times Square area."

As I walked to the Bible Society building, I prayed, "Lord, if You want me to check out this Lamb's place, please confirm it."

"I wish we could help you," the manager said, "but New York Bible Society policy doesn't permit us to work with individuals, only with recognized churches and organizations. I'm sorry." Disappointed but not surprised, I turned to leave when a young man behind the counter called, "Hey, brother, how's it going?"

When he learned I'd been spending my days in

the Times Square area, he said, "There's a new place over there. It's called The Lamb or something like that. Some Christians just took it over. You ought to check it out."

■ ■ ■

The young lady behind the desk introduced herself as Dianne. "Welcome to The Lamb's," she said with a warm smile. "Take a look around. The sanctuary's on the third floor."

I wandered through the building for several minutes, located the sanctuary, said a quick prayer, and headed back to the lobby. Dianne treated me like an old friend. She told me about The Lamb's Manhattan Church of the Nazarene and how the pastor had been challenging the congregation to take New York City for Jesus. She had my interest.

■ ■ ■ ■ ■ ■

Searching her pocket, Diane fished out a dollar bill and handed it to me with an understanding smile.

■ ■ ■ ■ ■ ■

"Bible study is tonight at 7:00," she said, "and you're invited."

"Thanks, I'll be back."

"Have you eaten?" she asked.

"No."

Searching her pocket, Dianne fished out a dollar bill and handed it to me with an understanding smile. Gratefully, I thanked her again and headed for the streets.

Seven came quickly. I made my way to the third-floor sanctuary and settled in as the congregation sang. Announcements included an invitation to the upcoming weekend revival and an appeal to support the church's Benevolence Ministry, an outreach to the homeless and poor. Then came the offering.

I was electrified by the message—overcoming the world through faith, which was taken from 1 John, chapter 5, the same passage and teaching as the last Bible study I'd attended in Pittsburgh. Coincidence? I doubted that.

After the service, Jerry, the man who'd made the appeal for the Benevolence Ministry, greeted me in the lobby. His broad grin and firm handshake encouraged me, but what followed took me by surprise. Releasing my hand, he reached into his pocket, pulled out a roll of bills, peeled off a 10 and slapped it into my hand. "Here, brother, the Lord wants you to have this."

Speechless, but grateful, I stumbled through a "thank you." Then out into the night, back to the streets I went, curious and excited, anxious to invite my street-people friends to the upcoming revival.

By Friday evening I think I invited everyone on 42nd Street. When I arrived at the church, I expected to see it packed with familiar faces. I saw none. Later that night I accelerated my efforts, but Saturday was no different. Sunday morning, only one of

The Lamb's Church of the Nazarene in New York City

my friends showed up. He left early, and I lost all enthusiasm.

Following the service, the congregation was invited for fellowship, coffee, and pastries. I would not be denied. I helped myself to plenty, and as I stuffed myself, I became lost in discouragement.

This is ridiculous, I thought. *I've been here two weeks, and no one's listening. I'm wasting my time. And where are You, Lord? I can't do this any longer. I'm human. I need food. And sleep. Maybe I misunderstood You.*

As I considered my options for returning to Pittsburgh, a hand rested on my shoulder and a vaguely familiar-sounding voice said, "Hello, brother. My name is Paul Moore." It was the pastor. He sat beside me and with genuine concern asked specific questions: Where are you from? How long have you been in New York? When did you last eat a balanced meal? How long since you slept in a bed?

My answers were brief and to the point. It would have been easy to manipulate his emotions but, even in my discouragement, I wanted the Lord's will, not mine.

When he'd heard enough, he arranged a bed for me in the basement and food for a week. "After you've rested," he said, "we'll talk again."

■ ■ ■ ■ ■ ■

I made myself useful, mopping floors, sorting clothes, scrubbing pots, organizing dishes.

■ ■ ■ ■ ■ ■

Sleep came easy. I must have been out for days.

Then I began to explore. Jerry's office was in the basement also, hidden inside a large room filled with give-away clothing. Across the hall was a small eat-in kitchen. Around the corner I discovered a large commercial kitchen where I met Gwen McGuire, chef for The Lamb's. Her delightful personality, West Indian accent, and obvious love for the Lord attracted me. Immediately, we became friends. She fed me well. I made myself useful, mopping floors, sorting clothes, scrubbing pots, organizing dishes.

When I met again with Pastor Moore, he invited

Gwen McGuire, chef for The Lamb's

me to extend my stay. I accepted. I really wanted to get to know these folks who embraced me like family. I worked with Jerry in the clothing room and with Gwen in the kitchen.

Weeks later in a letter to my folks, I summarized my activities since leaving home. When I checked the calendar to determine my arrival date at The Lamb's, I was stunned and began to weep. The direction to The Lamb's, Dianne's warm welcome, her dollar for lunch, the Bible study in 1 John, the invitation to the revival, Jerry and the $10 bill, my entire introduction to The Lamb's had all happened on October 27, my birthday. As I wept, the Lord spoke softly to my heart: *You forgot, but I did not. Happy birthday, son. Welcome to your new home.*

8
I Killed My Son

Along with New York, ministry at The Lamb's captured my heart. The six-story building on West 44th Street offered many opportunities to learn and to serve. In addition to the Benevolence Ministry, options included a restaurant on the first floor and a banquet hall on the second floor. The sanctuary/theater was located on three; the balcony and several offices on four. The upper two levels served as home for about 30 to 40 single Christians; men on five, ladies on six.

The Lamb's was a place to dream, where the Holy Spirit was free to tap the skills and utilize the talents and creative energy of willing "dare saints," as Pastor Moore called us. Ministry at The Lamb's wore many hats: the church, the residential community, evangelism in bars and singles clubs, contemporary Christian music concerts, Christian theater, a restaurant, and outreach to the neighborhood, the poor, and the homeless, to name a few. My calling was to the latter. I spent most of my time assisting Jerry with the Benevolence Ministry.

Thirteen days on the streets without food or sleep had seemed unfair and like an eternity. Looking back, however, it all began to make sense. Through this unique cross-cultural training program on homelessness, the Lord had been preparing me for ministry

Joe praying a blessing for a meal in the
Crisis Care program at The Lamb's

in an unusual mission field populated by street people. Having been where they were, I understood. I could relate. And I knew the Answer. What I couldn't have imagined just a few weeks before had now become my passion: ministry to the homeless in New York City.

A few months after my arrival, Jerry left The Lamb's, and the faith-supported Benevolence Ministry, later renamed Crisis Care, was turned over to me. We always had enough—donated clothing and the volunteers to sort it, restaurant leftovers supplied by Gwen to feed our frequent homeless visitors in the small basement kitchen, and vouchers for shelter at the Kingston Hotel, an inexpensive men's facility several blocks east.

Early on I developed a habit of seeking out old friends on 42nd Street. Often I found new ones, such as Tiny. At 6 feet 4 inches tall, he wasn't hard to spot. Neither was his drinking problem. Tiny seemed interested in the gospel at times but refused help with his addiction until the day we learned of a detox facility several miles upstate. Tiny wanted to go.

We scraped up enough money for a bus ticket and walked to the Port Authority. I saw him off and started home. But as I crossed 8th Avenue on that busy Friday evening, I had a strong sense the Lord had something more for me to do, someone He wanted me to talk with. People crowded the wide sidewalks, rushing in every direction. Finding even a familiar face in this crowd would be almost impossible.

■ ■ ■ ■ ■ ■

"You!" he commanded, staggering toward me, aiming his finger directly at my face. "I wanna talk to you."

■ ■ ■ ■ ■ ■

Jesus, if You want me to talk with someone, please show me who. And, Lord, please confirm it by allowing us to make eye contact, a connection usually avoided by New Yorkers.

The answer came swiftly. There, about 30 feet away, emerging from a crowd of hundreds and looking straight into my eyes, was my next assignment.

"You!" he commanded, staggering toward me, aiming his finger directly at my face. "I wanna talk to you."

I'd never seen him before. His name was Bill. Obviously drunk and probably homeless, neither condition interfered with his ability to quote scripture. The more we talked, the more apparent it became: Bill knew the Word.

Puzzled, I said, "You know this stuff. Why are you out here living like this?"

He talked in circles at first and then said, "God won't forgive me. He *can't* forgive me!"

"He can and He *will* forgive you. You just need to ask Him."

"You don't understand," he argued. "He could *never* forgive me!"

"If you're sincerely sorry and ask Him, He'll forgive you. There's nothing you could have done that He won't forgive."

"No, no. You don't understand," he growled, struggling to find his next words. Then almost in a whisper, "I . . . I . . . I killed my son."

Surprised but confident, I responded. "It's OK. The Lord will forgive you. It's OK."

"It's *OK?*" he screamed, grabbing me by the collar and pushing me against the wall. "It's *OK?* I *killed* my *son!* It's *not* OK!"

Startled by his anger, I prayed for words. "Bill, God knows your pain. He knows your heart; He knows you're sorry. Remember, His Word promises, 'If we confess our sins, he is faithful and just and will forgive us our sins and purify us from all unrighteousness.'* That's the truth. God gives you His Word. He cannot lie. He *will* forgive you, just ask Him."

Slowly, he released my collar, his anger subsiding, his eyes softening. "You really think He could forgive me? You think He *would* forgive *me?*"

"I *know* He will, Bill. Let's just ask Him."

■ ■ ■ ■ ■ ■

"Did . . . did you feel me just get forgiven?"

■ ■ ■ ■ ■ ■

Hesitantly, Bill took my hands. Oblivious to the crowd around us, we bowed our heads and prayed. I don't know exactly what happened, but in the middle of that prayer, at the exact moment Bill humbly asked for God's forgiveness, I felt a sensation similar to what a person might experience when the elevator floor seems to drop out from beneath them.

When we finished praying, Bill appeared shaken. He looked quizzically into my eyes and asked, "Did . . . did you *feel* me just get forgiven?"

"Yes," I said without hesitation, " I did feel you get forgiven."

"Oh, thank you," he said over and over again as he wept joyfully and embraced me. "I'm forgiven. I can't believe it. Thank you. Thank God I'm forgiven!"

Later I learned that at the time of his son's death Bill was a university professor.

---

*1 John 1:9

9
Happy Mother's Day

We were constantly searching for ways to reach more people with the gospel. About a year after my arrival, Gwen and I began a weekly meal program for the poor and homeless. When the food was served, I'd share the gospel with our guests.

We had no problem attracting folks to the dining room. Attracting them to church, however, was another matter. They seldom showed up. This concern prompted a visit with the Jewish owner of the Kingston Hotel. I asked permission to begin holding worship services there. To my surprise, he agreed. The following Sunday in a room just off the first-floor lobby with a congregation of 10, we launched the Kingston Hotel Church of the Nazarene, an experiment that lasted two years.

During that same period, Pastor Moore preached a stirring message from Luke's gospel. He spoke about reaching out to those who cannot give in return: "But when you give a banquet, invite the poor, the crippled, the lame, the blind" (Luke 14:13).

Challenged, Gwen and I put together the first annual Thanksgiving Day "Banquet for God" celebration. We handed out 200 formal invitations to street

Some of the "special" guests for the Banquet
for God celebration on Thanksgiving Day

Tuxedoed maître d's greeted guests who
came to the Banquet for God

people around Times Square. Volunteer offers and contributions poured in. One gift was designated to hire a limousine to search the city for guests in need of transportation to the banquet.

More than 150 guests were greeted by tuxedoed maître d's and escorted to linen-clad tables dressed with our finest china and silver. Countless volunteers helped prepare and serve a Thanksgiving Day feast fit for the King. Others provided the entertainment. That day a Lamb's tradition began that continued for more than 20 years.

About the same time, a young single gal arrived in New York. She'd come at the invitation of a friend to visit the city, find a job, and check out The Lamb's. She was searching for evidence of authentic Christianity at work in the world. She found it at The Lamb's, and soon Marilyn Davis moved in with the single adult community there. Marilyn's winsome smile and pleasant personality immediately attracted me. But I had no interest in a relationship, nor did I have the time to pursue one.

The ministry was growing more demanding; lunch program attendance increased as did requests for clothing, shelter, counseling, and referrals. Volunteers, including Marilyn, assisted in their spare time, but we needed steady help. The Lord sent Jim, who held a master's degree in social work and offered his services as a full-time volunteer for the next two years. With Jim's help we could handle the increasing demands.

Over the years many had accepted Christ as Savior and Lord, but without a strong foundation the commitment was short-lived. We responded by developing a residential program for homeless men who were serious about changing their lives and whom we could disciple. We converted an unused basement room into a small dormitory, labeled it the "Crash Pad," and took in our first six residents. The new program showed signs of success but demanded much more time and effort than we had anticipated. Six new Christians, all with a street-life mentality and no concept of curfews and boundaries, brought challenges, sometimes 24 hours a day. As the ministry intensified, so did the stress, and the opportunity for a break was most welcome.

■ ■ ■

About mid-May my friend Ted called. He was passing through New York on his way to Pittsburgh. "I'm sure your folks would love to see you," he said, "and besides we'll be there for Mother's Day. Why not come along for the ride? I'll be back this way in 8 or 10 days, and the round-trip won't cost you anything." The decision was not difficult.

Jim and B. J. Weber, The Lamb's associate pastor, agreed to look after my Crisis Care responsibilities. Ted and I headed for Pittsburgh.

Time with family is always special, and this occasion was no different. The highlight occurred on Mother's Day. As I sat in the kitchen alone with Mom, the opportunity arose to discuss my faith, usually taboo in her house. I shared stories of my recent adventures and about the Christ who was behind them. She listened intently.

"Mom, consider this. As a Catholic you believe Jesus is God's Son, right?"

"Yes."

"And you assume He lives in your heart, right?"

"Yes."

"Well, as I understand it, He stands at our heart's door and knocks, waiting for a sincere invitation to enter. He's not automatically in there because we're good people or because we belong to a certain denomination. So, if I'm right, inviting Him into your heart on purpose would eliminate any doubt that He's there. If I'm wrong, you've lost nothing. You've simply invited the Lord you love to draw closer."

The argument made sense, and we prayed. Happy Mother's Day, Mom.

10

The Man's Gonna Shoot You

On the return to New York, Ted decided I needed a wristwatch. It was hard to convince him otherwise, so I became the proud owner of a high-end Timex digital with all the bells and whistles. Literally.

Ted dropped me off at The Lamb's. It was good to be back home. The city's fast pace stimulated me as did the ministry. Yet after only two weeks I was ready for a break—if only for a few hours.

Bible study would begin in 30 minutes, but I'd had it for the day. With two hours of daylight remaining, I decided to visit Bryant Park, a large patch of "green" that shares an entire block with the New York Public Library. Surely I could cut one Wednesday evening service.

Visiting the park that evening was the typical array of joggers, musicians, chess players, pet walkers, book readers, and the like. I found an unoccupied bench and stretched out. Blotting out the noise, I gazed skyward through the leaves of huge sycamores. Slowly the stress began to lift.

When a young man approached and asked to join me, I was ready. "Sure," I said, sitting up, recognizing a perfect opportunity to share my faith.

Only seconds into our conversation, a loud

voice interrupted. I attempted to ignore it, but the volume increased with urgency. As the young man beside me disengaged, I realized we were surrounded, and the blaring voice was directed toward me.

"Gimme all ya got," ordered a man, pointing a pistol at my face. The sudden intrusion didn't register at first. Surely this was not happening.

"Take his watch," he commanded the young man by my side.

I'd been set up. Surrounded by six men, ranging in age from about 15 to 25, I was defenseless.

"You don't need to be doing this." I said. "Jesus can show you a . . ."

"Shut up 'n' gimme me your wallet!" he screamed.

■ ■ ■ ■ ■ ■

Wisdom said, "Cooperate." Reluctantly, I handed him my wallet.

■ ■ ■ ■ ■ ■

When I tried again to persuade him, the oldest-looking one in the group spoke up. "Ah, you don't understand. This man has a *gun*, an' he's gonna *shoot* you. Just give him what he wants, an' you won't git hurt."

Although I struggled with the principle, the odds were clearly in their favor, and wisdom said, "Cooperate." Reluctantly, I handed him my wallet.

When the young man beside me attempted to

take my new Timex, I yanked my arm away with an attitude. "You're not *taking* my watch," I announced. "I'll give it to you." Somehow that seemed to help. As I removed the watch and handed it over, the gunman finished with my wallet. He'd found $17.

"Dat's all ya got?" he yelled. "Seventeen bucks? I oughta shoot ya jest fo' dat!" He threw the empty wallet at my feet, and all six men scattered, each in a different direction.

I sat stunned. It was still broad daylight. The park was filled with people, several occupying the benches on either side of me, not 15 feet away. They'd witnessed it all, yet no one said a word.

Shaken, I walked back to The Lamb's, trying to process my emotions, certain I'd miss no future Bible studies.

11
Homeless Again

Slowly I recovered from the robbery. Forgiveness was the key. Gradually my faith continued to mature.

Creative freedom allowed ministry at The Lamb's to develop constantly. We were serving lunch five days a week at the restaurant, and with help from many volunteer musicians, we sponsored a Christian coffeehouse on weekends. New ideas came often.

Aware that multiple thousands of people regularly visit Times Square, especially on weekends, an idea began to form around the coffeehouse tables. Several of the musicians and I decided to take a band to Duffy Square Park, a tiny but strategically located triangle of land bordered by Broadway, 7th Avenue, and 46th Street, one of the busiest intersections in NYC. We secured a permit from the city, borrowed power from a local business, and we were ready to rock 'n' roll.

Every Friday night for two years, weather permitting, we set up in Duffy Square. The musicians played, and between sets I preached. The music drew hundreds. The preaching wasn't popular, but at every concert, people requested prayer. Once in a while someone prayed to receive Christ. On several

Joe speaking at Duffy Square Park, NYC

Saturdays we took the same idea to Central Park with similar results.

As time went on, Pastor Moore was called to pastor a church in California. The Lamb's associate pastors Michael Christensen, B. J. Weber, and I han-

Service in Central Park, NYC

dled interim responsibilities until Orville Jenkins Jr. and his wife, Nancy, arrived to assume leadership.

Under the new direction of Rev. Jenkins, the parsonage was sold and proceeds were invested in restoring The Lamb's building to its original historic state. Everyone pitched in. Night and day we worked. Help came from everywhere: the congregation, Lamb's residents and staff, Work and Witness teams, and the half-dozen former street people residing in the Crash Pad. It was a monumental task, but worth the effort. The entire building was slowly transformed into a beautifully new, historically accurate, more functional facility.

Joe *(left)* with the other associate pastors at The Lamb's, B. J. Weber *(center)* and Michael Christiansen

This was an exciting and pivotal time for me personally. Over the years I had tried to patch things up with Dolly. By now we were friends, but she'd re-married and had a child, which closed the door to any future hopes I may have had.

And then there was Marilyn. She'd been living at The Lamb's for four years. She worked in the church office and volunteered often for ministry. She consistently demonstrated a servant's heart, a sincere compassion for the poor, and a deep love for Jesus. During the renovation project, we worked to-gether often. I learned she'd been an MK (mission-ary kid) in Japan. I enjoyed her company, and before I knew it, I was falling in love.

But there was really nowhere to take the rela-tionship. I was broke. I hadn't needed, wanted, or re-ceived a paycheck since I left Pittsburgh for Santa Fe some nine years earlier. And besides I had other work to do.

■ ■ ■

With summer came the inspiration to leave my responsibilities at The Lamb's and take time off for a kind of refresher course. We called it a street-life sab-batical. The idea? To live again among the homeless, to become one of them, to remember what hungry, tired, and forgotten feel like. Also, learning more about New York's social service delivery system, we could improve our ministry to the homeless at The Lamb's.

B. J. and I planned to touch base intermittently for updates somewhere in the city. He usually brought along a piece of fruit and a few dollars—"just in case." Sometimes he'd bring Marilyn.

The first two weeks I worked my way toward the Lower East Side, home of the Bowery, the famous skid row of the city. As I'd done years before, I attempted to sleep in parks and in the lobbies of public transportation buildings, again with little success. Along the way I shared my faith with anyone who'd listen.

Together with hundreds of other homeless people, I waited hours in the St. Francis breadline for a breakfast: two baloney sandwiches and a cup of coffee. They were out of coffee.

When I finally made it to the Lower East Side, I visited the Social Services Department where I was assigned a social worker, who was quite interested in my adventure. He was also concerned for my safety and requested periodic reports. He issued me a 30-day ticket for meals at the "Muni," the city's Municipal Shelter. Then came a voucher for one change of clothes for the month and another for a room at the Union Hotel—a slight improvement over my previous homeless experience.

■ ■ ■ ■ ■ ■

The education I received that summer was priceless.

■ ■ ■ ■ ■ ■

My room was one of about 40 identical cubicles arranged side-by-side in several rows within a larger room. The narrow door opened into a 4' x 7' space. It was better than the streets.

The education I received that summer was priceless. It would take another entire book to properly tell the story. It is sufficient to say, however, that the Lord used that time in my life to shape within me a more comprehensive vision for ministry among the homeless. One small facet of that vision was fashioned through Nathan, a personable 30-year-old recovering addict I'd met at the hotel.

Nathan introduced me to the program from which he'd graduated and which now employed him. It was a kind of large-scale, secular crash-pad program, designed to help wayward men get their lives together and eventually become full-time city employees. The program provided housing for its 60 participants on the second floor of the Muni. Assistance included drug and alcohol detox, mental health services, group therapy, individual counseling, recreation, and a small stipend. In return, participants carried out work details in and around the six-story facility. These were stimulating ideas that I hoped I could use some day.

After eight weeks I'd accomplished my goal. Now, more aware of the resources available and more sensitive to the needs of the homeless, I was better equipped to assist them and ready to return to The Lamb's. The experiment had worked.

There was another benefit. My meetings with B. J. had been refreshing. But even more refreshing were the times when Marilyn accompanied him. Sometimes she and I slipped away for a romantic

Welcome-back celebration after Joe's street-life sabbatical

cruise on the Staten Island Ferry. For 25 cents we sailed from the tip of Manhattan across the bay, past the Statue of Liberty, to experience the cool breeze in our faces and the quieter, slower pace of Staten Island. We walked through the streets, sharing our hearts and picking mulberries from a favorite tree. Hours later we hopped back on the ferry and returned to our lives in the city.

12
Beyond What We Ask or Imagine

Throughout that next year my relationship with Marilyn deepened, and the desire to be married grew stronger. Trusting the Lord, we set the date for November.

Still, we had nothing. Marilyn was working for very little as The Lamb's secretary, and I was living by faith. The Lord knew our situation; certainly Marilyn's great-uncle Herb did not.

Herb had lived in New Jersey for years and been alone since his wife died. Several months before the wedding we visited him to share the news of our engagement. During our visit he handed Marilyn a small box.

"I want you to have this," he said. It was a beautiful diamond ring, a treasured keepsake he'd given to his beloved many years before. Overwhelmed we gratefully accepted his gift of love.

That was the beginning.

When honeymoon plans to drive cross-country fell through, we were out of ideas.

"Well, wherever you decide to go," offered a friend at The Lamb's, "let me know. I want to cover your plane fare. Have you thought about Puerto Rico?"

I hadn't even thought about the Bronx.

Two weeks before the wedding, Marilyn's folks, missionaries to Japan, arrived in New York. When her father, Frank, heard about the offer for plane fare, he called a pastor friend in—you guessed it—Puerto Rico! He encouraged us to come, offered the use of a car, and arranged for us to spend several days in a beachfront condominium. No charge.

■ ■ ■ ■ ■ ■

For three wonderful weeks we explored this tropical paradise, guests of the Lord.

■ ■ ■ ■ ■ ■

Family and friends came from several states for our wedding at The Lamb's. Church friends catered a spectacular reception; Gwen took care of the cake. The Lamb's staff provided a night at an upscale hotel overlooking Central Park. Other gifts included ample cash. The floodgates had opened.

At the San Juan airport, over a cup of Puerto Rican coffee, the pastor introduced us to the culture. Along with keys to both the condominium and a red '64 Mustang, he handed us a map of the island and turned us loose. For three wonderful weeks we explored this tropical paradise, guests of the Lord.

When we returned to the States, we spent some

Joe and Marilyn at their wedding reception

time at a retreat center before returning to The Lamb's. Pastor Jenkins offered me a job, my first paid position in nearly 10 years.

I accepted!

Epilogue

When Jesus lifted me
from that dark and hopeless place,
and brought me into the light,
I could never have imagined
what He had in store.
He grew my faith,
opened my eyes, and changed my heart.
He redirected my career
and led me to the mission field—
the New York City streets.
He introduced me to the Church of the Nazarene,
trained me for ministry,
provided a wife and eventually a family.
The story continues;
it's not yet complete.

"Being confident of this, that he who
began a good work in you will carry it on
to completion until the day of Christ Jesus"
(Phil. 1:6).

Afterword

And there is more. Much more!

Joe Colaizzi's dramatic and powerful story does not end with his marriage to Marilyn and his ministry at the Lamb's Manhattan Church of the Nazarene. The Almighty God, who Joe dearly loves and serves, has directed his life to another mission in Kansas City.

Joe's adventure of faith is to be continued, and you can read the rest of the story in a sequel next year.

In the meantime, celebrate what the Lord has done in the life of a man who believed he was Satan, lifting him from a life of alcohol and drugs, and transforming him to be a minister of the gospel and a rescuer of broken and hurting people.

—Wes Eby, editor